For the Teacher

This reproducible study guide to use in conjunction with the novel *The City of Ember* consists of lessons for guided reading. Written in chapter-by-chapter format, the guide contains a synopsis, pre-reading activities, vocabulary and comprehension exercises, as well as extension activities to be used as follow-up to the novel.

In a homogeneous classroom, whole class instruction with one title is appropriate. In a heterogeneous classroom, reading groups should be formed: each group works on a different novel at its own reading level. Depending upon the length of time devoted to reading in the classroom, each novel, with its guide and accompanying lessons, may be completed in three to six weeks.

Begin using NOVEL-TIES for reading development by distributing the novel and a folder to each child. Distribute duplicated pages of the study guide for students to place in their folders. After examining the cover and glancing through the book, students can participate in several pre-reading activities. Vocabulary questions should be considered prior to reading a chapter; all other work should be done after the chapter has been read. Comprehension questions can be answered orally or in writing. The classroom teacher should determine the amount of work to be assigned, always keeping in mind that readers must be nurtured and that the ultimate goal is encouraging students' love of reading.

The benefits of using NOVEL-TIES are numerous. Students read good literature in the original, rather than in abridged or edited form. The good reading habits, formed by practice in focusing on interpretive comprehension and literary techniques, will be transferred to the books students read independently. Passive readers become active, avid readers.

Novel-Ties® are printed on recycled paper.

SYNOPSIS

The builders of Ember left instructions in a box that was set to open in two hundred and twenty years. Each successive mayor was to keep the box a secret and hand it down to a successor. Unfortunately, the box became lost in the back of the seventh mayor's closet, where it opened automatically, unnoticed by anyone.

In Ember there is complete darkness except for a few hours each day when the electricity is working. With the generator failing, there are numerous blackouts and stored supplies are running out. Twelve-year-old Doon Harrow wants to be an electrician's helper or Pipeworks laborer in order to fix the generator and thus save Ember. Lina Mayfleet desperately wants to be a messenger. On Assignment Day, when Doon draws messenger and Lina draws Pipeworks laborer, the two happily trade jobs.

On her first day as messenger, Lina receives a strange message to deliver to the mayor from an odd-looking person named Looper. Meanwhile, working in the damp tunnels deep underground, Doon manages to find the generator but cannot understand how it works.

Lina's job takes her to the greenhouses to see Clary, a co-worker and friend of her late father's. There a man named Sadge talks about his failed venture into the dark Unknown Regions that surround Ember. The lack of movable light now makes such an undertaking impossible.

Lina, who lives with Granny and her baby sister Poppy, discovers a beautifully-made box when Granny rummages through her closet. She rescues the document that was inside from Poppy, who has already torn and chewed it. Convinced it is important, Lina pastes the pieces together as best she can. After decoding the word "Pipeworks," she goes to Doon for help. The instructions mention a locked door which Doon remembers seeing in the Pipeworks. When the children investigate, they hear someone enter and leave the locked room. Lina gets a glimpse of a familiar, odd-looking figure—Looper.

After Granny dies, Lina and Poppy move in with their neighbor Mrs. Murdo. For sympathy, Lina seeks out her friend Lizzie, who works at the Supply Depot. Evasive and guarded, Lizzie drops some cans of food that were supposedly depleted from the storerooms. Lina soon finds out that Lizzie's boyfriend, Looper, gave them to her.

One day Doon finds the door to the stockroom open, allowing him to see a huge stash of supplies inside and the mayor asleep in the middle of it all. Having concluded that Looper is providing the mayor with ill-gotten goods, Lina and Doon inform the guards about the mayor's corruption.

After Clary tells Lina that one of the words in the document means "the exit," Lina and Doon confer to decode more of the instructions, which lead them to a dark room in the Pipeworks. There they find boxes of candles and matches. Once they realize how to use the "movable lights," they go back in the room and discover boats. The way out of Ember is by boat on the river.

The children's plan to announce their discovery at the annual Singing is thwarted when guards come to arrest them for spreading vicious rumors. Hiding in the school, they write to Clary explaining how to leave Ember. Lina will deliver the message and then leave with Doon. Unfortunately, Lina is captured and brought before the mayor. Managing to escape during a blackout, she races home to get Poppy and meets Doon in the Pipeworks. They leave on a treacherous boat ride, which ends with the discovery of a path and a notebook. A sign welcomes refugees from Ember and indicates they must climb for several hours. At the end of the climb, the children follow a light to the outside world.

As they read the notebook, the children discover that the builders sent a group of elderly people and babies to inhabit Ember so that people would not disappear from the earth. Exploring further, Lina and Doon look down a cliff and see Ember below. Since Lina never left the note for Clary, the children drop it down below. The book ends as the note falls to the ground in front of Mrs. Murdo.

BACKGROUND INFORMATION

Science Fiction

Science fiction is narrative based on the application of elements of science and technology to imaginary situations. It can be set in the future, the past, or another dimension. Common subjects for science fiction include space travel, invasions from space, time travel, and future societies.

The beginnings of science fiction lie in the tales of such European authors as Mary Shelly, Jules Verne, and H.G. Wells. Shelly's publication of *Frankenstein* in 1818 is considered by some to be the first science fiction novel. Verne is credited with refining the genre during the 1860s in such works as *A Journey to the Center of the Earth*. Wells, one of Verne's most successful imitators, wrote such famous novels as *The Time Machine*, which was published in 1895.

In the United States, the roots of science fiction can be found in the supernatural works of Nathaniel Hawthorne and Ambrose Bierce in the mid to late 1800s. By the turn of the century, the audience for science fiction had greatly increased, perhaps because of the fascination with the boom in technology. As a distinct category, science fiction came into its own in April 1926 with the publication of Hugo Gernsback's *Amazing Stories*, the first magazine devoted solely to science fiction. One of the most prominent of today's science fiction awards, the Hugo, bears his name.

The next important influence on the genre was John Wood Campbell, who was hired in 1937 as editor of *Astounding Stories*, a famous science fiction magazine in which such noted authors as Isaac Asimov and Robert Heinlein published some of the their works. Campbell's insistence on high literary standards contributed to the reputation of the genre.

After World War II, science fiction began to change; there was more of an emphasis on detailed, accurate descriptions of scientific devices and processes. There was also more concern with how scientific change would affect our society. The genre became more respectable, and science fiction books joined the ranks of science fiction magazines. Established science fiction writers such as Robert Heinlein, Ursula LeGuin, and Ray Bradbury began writing quality science fiction for young adults. They were joined by authors writing primarily for this audience, such as Andre Norton, Madeleine L'Engle, Virginia Hamilton, and John Christopher.

From the 1950s to the present, science fiction has greatly expanded its outlets and readership. Science fiction continues its popularity in films, television shows, and science fiction clubs as well as books.

Electricity

Electricity is a form of energy that occurs when the balancing force between protons and electrons (basic elements of every atom) is upset by an outside force. This outside force generates millions of free-flowing electrons whose movements create force fields and generate energy from motion. The electrons transmit an electrical charge through solid matter, such as metal, to produce an electric current.

An electric generator is a device used to convert mechanical energy into electrical energy. A generator makes electricity with the help of a turbine by moving a magnet inside a coil of wire. This produces an alternating current (AC current), which flows rapidly back and forth in the wire.

Water is used to power generators in hydroelectric plants. For such a plant, rivers are dammed to make a source of falling water. Masses of water collect in a hydro dam, which artificially raises the water level. This water is channeled through tunnels in the dam and then falls with incredible power onto the blades of a turbine, causing them to turn. The turbine's energy sets generators in motion, which then produce electricity.

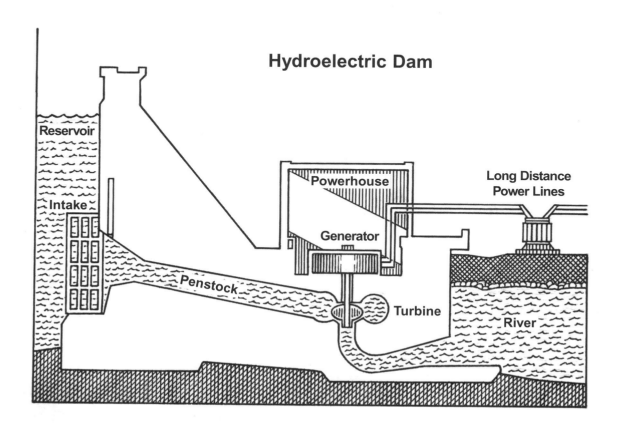

Hydroelectric Dam

PRE-READING QUESTIONS AND ACTIVITIES

1. Preview the book by reading the title and the author's name and by looking at the picture on the cover. What do you think this book will be about? Will it be serious or humorous? When and where does it take place?

2. Look at the map of the city of Ember at the beginning of the novel. Where is the subterranean river? What lies beyond the beehives and greenhouses? As you read, trace the action of the story on the map.

3. Read the Background Information on Science Fiction that you will find on page three of this study guide. What do you think are the most important elements of a work of science fiction? Use a chart, such as the one below, to list the most important elements of a science fiction story. As you read, record examples of these elements and the pages on which you find them.

Elements of Science Fiction	Page Number	*The City of Ember*

4. Do some research to find biographical information about Jeanne DuPrau, the author of this novel. Learn about her professional life and family life. What do you think was the inspiration for *The City of Ember*?

5. Imagine that you can get into a time machine and travel hundreds of years into the future. What do you think you would see? Would things be better or worse than they are now?

6. What, if any, are valid reasons for a leader to limit the freedoms and rights of citizens? What dangers can this lead to? Give examples from history to support your response.

7. **Cooperative Learning Activity:** In a small cooperative learning group, discuss environmental and political issues that threaten our world today. What might result if these issues are not resolved? Compare your conclusions with those of other groups.

8. Read the Background Information on electricity on page four of this study guide. How do you think daily life would be changed if electricity was only available for one hour each day?

Pre-Reading Questions and Activities (cont.)

9. The title of this novel is *The City of Ember*. An ember is a piece of coal, wood, or other material that is still glowing in the ashes of a fire. On the word web below, write a word in each circle that relates to the word *ember*. Then compare your diagram with those of your classmates. What do you imagine the city of Ember will be like?

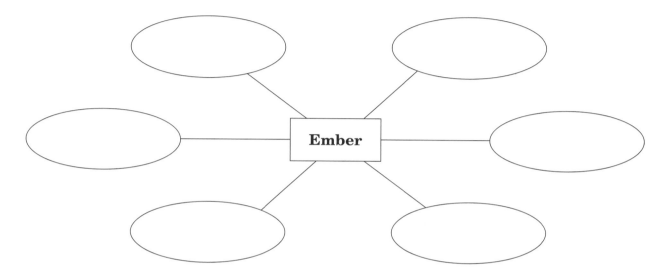

THE INSTRUCTIONS, CHAPTERS 1, 2

Vocabulary: Draw a line from each word on the left to its definition on the right. Then use the numbered words to fill in the blanks in the sentences below.

1. endeavor
2. successor
3. frayed
4. labyrinth
5. scavengers
6. plummeting
7. reverberating
8. disreputable

a. worn along the edge, usually referring to a fabric
b. falling straight down
c. serious effort over time
d. echoing
e. not respectable
f. maze
g. one who follows another in office
h. people who search through discarded items for something of value

. . . .

1. I offered to repair the _____ collar of my sister's favorite blouse.

2. Afraid that I would come into contact with _____ companions, my mother tried to send me to a school in another neighborhood.

3. The book came _____ to the ground after accidentally being pushed out the window.

4. John Adams was Washington's _____ as president.

5. We needed a guide to lead us through the _____ of caves.

6. The deep _____ tones of the organ bounced off the walls of the church, filling the building with its sound.

7. To become an Olympic figure skater is a major _____ that will take years of hard work.

8. If I put the old furniture out at the curb, it won't be long before _____ come to take it away.

Read to find out about life in the city of Ember.

Questions:

1. How did the builders of Ember make sure that the instructions would not be seen for two hundred and twenty years?

2. How did the builders plan to keep the box safe and secret?

The Instructions, Chapters 1, 2 (cont.)

3. What went wrong with the builders' plan?

4. Why is electricity especially important for the city of Ember?

5. Why does the mayor come to the classroom on the last day of school? Why is Lina disappointed when she picks "Pipeworks laborer" as her job?

6. Why does Doon change jobs with Lina?

7. Why is Lina surprised by Doon's criticism of the city of Ember?

8. Why is no one in Ember sure of the hour, day of the week, or year?

Questions for Discussion:

1. Why do you think Lina and many others in the city of Ember do not rebel against the life they must accept?

2. Why do you think a society would put a twelve-year-old to work instead of continuing his or her education?

3. What does the role of messenger reveal about the city of Ember?

4. Who might be the "Believers," and what do you think they were doing in Garn Square?

5. How does Mrs. Polster's way of teaching compare to that in your own classes? Do you agree that there is always a clear choice between right and wrong?

6. What would bother you most about living in Ember? Is there anything you would like about living there?

Literary Element: Setting

Setting refers to the place and time in which the events in a work of fiction occur. What is the setting of this novel?

_____

How important do you think the setting will be to this story?

_____

What details of the setting make the story seem real?

_____

_____

The Instructions, Chapters 1, 2 (cont.)

Literary Devices:

I. *Simile*—A simile is a figure of speech in which two unlike objects are compared using the words "like" or "as." For example:

> . . . his [the mayor's] heavy cheeks folded like drapes.

What is being compared in this simile?

_____

How does this help you to visualize the mayor?

_____

_____

II. *Metaphor*—A metaphor is a figure of speech in which a comparison between two unlike objects is suggested or implied. For example:

> Somewhere inside her, a black worm of dread stirred.

To what is the dread being compared?

_____

How does this help to convey Lina's feelings?

_____

_____

III. *Flashback*—A flashback is a scene or a series of scenes showing events that happened at an earlier time. Indicate where the flashback begins and ends in Chapter 2. What purpose does this flashback serve?

_____

_____

_____

_____

Writing Activity:

The occupations of Lina and her friends are decided by a chance draw of a slip of paper from a bag. Imagine that you are one of the young people picking a job. Describe the job you would want most and tell what you like about it. Then describe the job you would want the least and tell why it would not suit you.

CHAPTERS 3 – 5

Vocabulary: Use the context to determine the meaning of the underlined word in each of the following sentences. Then compare your definition with a dictionary definition.

1. I couldn't sleep because there was a <u>raucous</u> party going on in the next apartment.
   Your definition_____

   Dictionary definition_____

2. The boat kept bouncing up and down and side to side as it sailed through the <u>turbulent</u> waters.
   Your definition_____

   Dictionary definition_____

3. The earthquake left a <u>chasm</u> into which the hut fell.
   Your definition_____

   Dictionary definition_____

4. Every member of the board was in <u>attendance</u> for the meeting.
   Your definition_____

   Dictionary definition_____

5. After running around in circles, the dog was <u>enmeshed</u> in the rope used to tie him to the tree.
   Your definition_____

   Dictionary definition_____

6. People often become <u>disagreeable</u> when they are tired.
   Your definition_____

   Dictionary definition_____

7. After she awoke from the surgery, she was speaking <u>incoherently</u>.
   Your definition_____

   Dictionary definition_____

Read to find out about Doon's first day on the job.

Chapters 3 – 5 (cont.)

Questions:

1. How does working as a Pipeworks laborer convince Doon that the city is in even worse shape than he had suspected?

2. Why is Doon's first look at the generator disappointing to him?

3. Why is it important to Doon to be the one to save the city?

4. Why does Lina ask Mrs. Murdo to check up on her grandmother during the day?

5. Why does the newly named job of trash sifter cause Lina to worry?

6. Why does Sadge come to the greenhouse in a state of panic?

7. Why does Clary give Lina a bean seed?

8. Why does Lina have trouble finding Poppy after she wanders away from the store?

9. Why don't the colored pencils bring Lina happiness?

Questions for Discussion:

1. Why do you think that nobody in Ember has been able to invent a movable light?

2. Do you believe that Sadge has gone mad in his pursuit of the Unknown Regions?

3. Do you think there is any hope for the city of Ember? If so, what might it be?

4. Is there anything about the plight of the city of Ember that is like the problems we have in our own cities today?

Literary Elements:

I. *Mood*—Mood is the overall atmosphere or feeling of a story. Happiness or sadness, terror or tranquility—mood can be any strong feeling or emotion the author creates, often by using descriptive details. Read the following passage:

> She began to tremble, and she felt the sinking and dissolving inside her that meant she was going to cry. Her legs gave way like wet paper and she slid down until she was sitting on the street, with her head on her knees. Trembling, her mind a wordless whirl of dread, she waited.

What mood is set by the passage?

_____

Underline those words that create this mood.

Chapters 3 – 5 (cont.)

II. *Characterization*—Characters in literature are revealed by what they say and do and by what others say about them. In a chart, such as the one below, list important information you have learned about some of the characters in the novel. Continue to fill in the chart as you read. You may also add more characters to the chart.

Character	Physical Appearance	Personality Traits
Lina		
Doon		
The mayor		
Clary		
Mrs. Murdo		

Literary Device: Personification

Personification is a literary device in which an author grants human qualities to inanimate objects. For example:

> But the darkness pressed against her and she couldn't summon her voice.

What is being personified?

_____

What is the effect?

_____

Science Connection:

Start a list of foods that are found in Ember and continue the list as you read on. Consider which foods are on the list and which are missing. Does anything surprise you? For example, why doesn't the greenhouse grow fruits or grains? Why is there no livestock?

Writing Activity:

Write about a time when you felt a hunger for something like Lina felt for the pencils. What did you want? Did you get it? If not, why? If so, what did it cost you?

CHAPTERS 6 – 8

Vocabulary: Choose a word from the Word Box to replace each underlined word or phrase with a word that has a similar meaning. Write the word you choose on the line below the sentence.

WORD BOX			
discontinued	ignited	incomprehensible	kiosks
disorderly	illegible	intact	unintended

1. People were selling goods from <u>small structures open at one or more sides</u>.

   _____

2. The message coming from the loudspeaker was <u>not able to be understood</u>.

   _____

3. Knocking down the vase was an <u>accidental</u> result of playing ball in the house.

   _____

4. Maria received her aunt's stamp collection <u>with nothing missing or injured</u>.

   _____

5. The police will make sure that the crowd does not get <u>rowdy</u>.

   _____

6. Because it was not popular, that model was <u>no longer manufactured</u>.

   _____

7. Your handwriting is <u>impossible to read</u>.

   _____

8. The spark from the campfire <u>set on fire</u> the dry leaves.

   _____

> Read to find out how the mayor responds to the blackout.

Questions:

1. Why do the people show anger toward the mayor at the town meeting?

2. What makes Lina think that the box from the closet contains something important?

3. Why don't Captain Fleery and the other Believers worry about the state of the city of Ember?

Chapters 6 – 8 (cont.)

4. What strategy do most of the people in Ember use to cope with the shortages and blackouts?

5. Why does Lina decide to take the document to Doon?

6. Why is Doon interested in the subject of fire?

Questions for Discussion:

1. What do you think is the nature of the instructions on the torn paper?

2. Do you agree with Doon's father that anger should be avoided because it always brings about unexpected consequences? Can anger ever be constructive?

3. What do you think the mayor has done with Lina's message?

4. Why do the people of Ember know so little about fire?

5. Why would the people of Ember not know common words such as *heaven, hog,* or *boat*?

6. How are the fictional Believers in the city of Ember like people in the real world?

7. How do you think Ember reached its present state?

Literary Devices:

I. *Personification*—What is being personified in the following passage?
    Fear had settled over the city.

    _____

    What mood does this create?

    _____

II. *Simile*—What is being compared in the following simile?
    Her heart began knocking at her chest like a fist at a door.

    _____

    Why is this an apt comparison?

    _____

Cooperative Learning Activity:

With a small group of your classmates, try to decode the document. Compare your results with those of other groups.

Writing Activity:

Write about a time when anger took hold of you and resulted in unintended consequences.

CHAPTERS 9 – 11

Vocabulary: Synonyms are words with similar meanings. Draw a line from each word in column A to its synonym in column B. Then use the words in column A to fill in the blanks in the sentences below.

	A			B
1.	sturdy		a.	carefully
2.	compartment		b.	spoiled
3.	methodically		c.	section
4.	unmistakable		d.	delicious
5.	tainted		e.	strolling
6.	sauntering		f.	strong
7.	delectable		g.	distinct

. . . .

1. Nobody can fail to recognize the _____ sound of a hyena.

2. My mother won a prize for her _____ apple pie.

3. You should wear _____ boots if you plan a long hike in the woods.

4. His reputation was _____ by rumors of dishonesty.

5. My wallet has one _____ for bills and another for coins.

6. The elderly couple was _____ across the park on a beautiful spring afternoon.

7. Bob _____ put together the pieces of his model airplane.

> Read to find out what happens when Lina shows Doon the document.

Questions:

1. How does Doon react when he sees Lina's document?

2. Why does Lina decide to go to the Pipeworks?

3. Why are Lina and Doon disappointed during their after-hours visit to the Pipeworks?

4. Why does Granny call Lina into her room in the middle of the night?

5. In what ways does Mrs. Murdo show she is "somewhere between a friend and a relative" to Lina?

Chapters 9 – 11 (cont.)

6.   How has life in Ember changed since the seven-minute power outage?

7.   Why does Lizzie try to avoid Lina when they see one another on the street?

8.   Why does Lina refuse to accept Lizzie's offer of more food in the future?

Questions for Discussion:

1.   Who do you think is the mysterious man who opened the locked door? What do you think is behind the door?

2.   If people go to work at the age of twelve, how do you think they get to be doctors?

3.   Do you agree with Lizzie or with Lina about using the secret supplies?

Literary Devices:

I.   *Irony*—Irony is a contrast between expectation and reality. Dramatic irony occurs when the reader knows something a character does not know. What is ironic about Lina using blue to color the sky in her picture?

_____

_____

II.   *Simile*—The author uses similes to describe illness. Rewrite each of the following examples using literal language without similes.

> . . . he [Lina's father] seemed to grow dim like a lamp losing power, and the sound of this breathing was like water gurgling through a clogged pipe.

_____

_____

> It [Granny's pulse] was fluttery, like a moth that has hurt itself and is flapping in crooked circles.

_____

_____

Why do you think the author uses similes instead of literal language for these descriptions?

Writing Activity:

Imagine that you are Mrs. Murdo. You have saved some paper for a journal. In a journal entry describe your feelings about Lina and Poppy. Tell why you invited them to live with you.

CHAPTERS 12 – 14

Vocabulary: Synonyms are words with similar meanings. Antonyms are words with opposite meanings. Place an "S" beside each pair of words that are synonyms. Place an "A" next to each pair of words that are antonyms. Then use the words from column I to fill in the blanks in the sentences below.

	I	II	A/S
1.	slogans	sayings	
2.	impatience	endurance	
3.	decipher	solve	
4.	egress	entrance	
5.	convoluted	simple	
6.	mottled	spotted	
7.	embedded	fixed	
8.	dim	bright	

1. According to the legend, Arthur removed the sword that was _____ in the stone.

2. Once you _____ the code, you will be able to read the message.

3. In the _____ light, we were unable to read the menu.

4. Advertisers use clever _____ so that you will remember to buy their products.

5. Once the door was locked, no other _____ was possible.

6. The girl's skin was _____ with small red marks from the measles.

7. When the singer failed to appear on stage, the crowd showed their _____ by clapping and stamping their feet.

8. The _____ path winds around streams and boulders.

Read to find out what Doon discovers in the locked room.

Chapters 12 – 14 (cont.)

Questions:

1. What does Doon discover when he opens the door to the locked room in Tunnel 351?

2. Why is it getting harder for people in Ember to put the problem of failing electricity out of their minds?

3. How does Doon's information about the store room relate to Looper?

4. How does Lina realize that Doon is her best friend?

5. Why does Lina go to see Clary?

6. In what ways does Clary give Lina new hope about the instructions?

7. Why does Doon have trouble sleeping after spending the evening with Lina?

8. How do Doon and Lina discover movable lights to guide them on their path?

9. What do Doon and Lina discover is the way out of Ember?

Questions for Discussion:

1. In your opinion, should Doon and Lina have told the guards about the mayor's corruption?

2. Do you think Doon and Lina will be able to reveal the way people can go beyond Ember at the Singing?

3. What does Clary mean when she tells Lina, "Everyone has some darkness inside"? What darkness, if any, have you detected in Lina and Doon?

Literary Device: Symbolism

A symbol in literature is a person, object, or event that represents an idea or set of ideas. What might the Believers symbolize?

_____

_____

_____

What does the encroaching darkness in Ember symbolize?

_____

_____

What might the germinating seed in Lina's room symbolize?

_____

_____

Chapters 12 – 14 (cont.)

Literary Elements:

I. *Conflict*—A conflict is a struggle between opposing forces. An external conflict is a character's struggle against an outside force, such as nature, society, or another person. An internal conflict is a personal struggle that takes place within a character's mind. In the chart below, list the conflicts that have occurred in the story so far. Indicate how some of these problems have been resolved. As you continue the story, add to the chart.

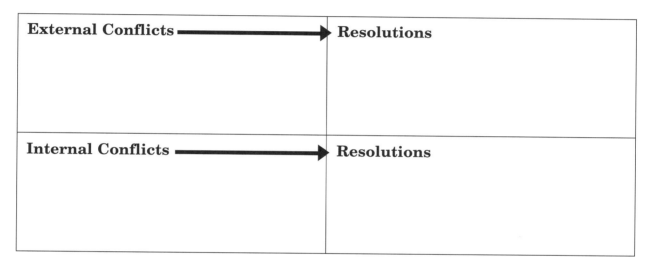

II. *Characterization*—Although Lina and Doon are alike in many ways, they are also different. Use a Venn diagram, such as the one below, to compare the two characters.

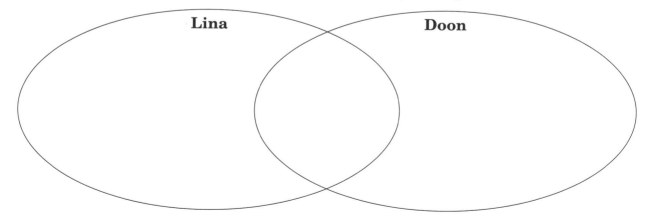

Writing Activity:

Using information from the Venn diagram, explain why Lina and Doon have developed a close friendship.

CHAPTERS 15 – 17

Vocabulary: Use the words in the Word Box and the clues below to complete the crossword puzzle.

WORD BOX
abundance
accomplice
curtly
defying
dispersing
enraged
impudence
ponderously
rummaged
tumult
unfurled

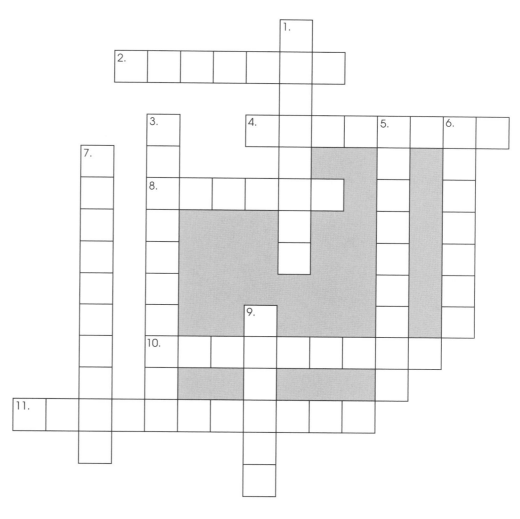

Across

2. resisting boldly or openly
4. searched thoroughly
8. in a rudely abrupt manner
10. shameless boldness
11. with difficulty

Down

1. unrolled
3. person who helps another do something wrong or illegal
5. plentiful supply
6. furious
7. scattering
9. violent disturbance; commotion

Read to find out what happens to hinder Doon and Lina's escape from Ember.

Chapters 15 – 17 (cont.)

Questions:

1. Why does Doon put off telling his father about the way out of Ember?

2. Why does Nammy Proggs direct the guards to the trash heaps?

3. Why do Doon and Lina decide to hide in the school?

4. Why won't Lina set her escape plan in motion immediately upon devising it with Doon?

5. How does Lina manage to escape from the mayor?

6. How does Lina know that Doon is on his way to the river?

7. Why does Doon leave a note on the kiosk?

8. How does Lina add risk to her escape from Ember?

Questions for Discussion:

1. Do you think Doon is being selfish when he doesn't share his plans with his father?

2. Do you agree with the mayor that curiosity is a dangerous and unhealthy quality? In what ways has curiosity helped Lina and Doon? In what ways has it put them in danger?

3. Do you think Lina should have taken Poppy with her? Why does having Poppy with her make Lina feel brave?

4. Do you think Lina and Doon will survive their trip and reach another city?

Literary Devices:

I. *Symbolism*—Why does the author include the storyline of a caterpillar that turned into a moth? What might Doon's caterpillar symbolize? In what way does this compare to Lina's bean sprout?

_____

_____

Chapters 15 – 17 (cont.)

II. *Cliffhanger*—A cliffhanger is a device borrowed from serialized silent films in which an episode ends at a moment of great tension or suspense. In literature, it usually appears at the end of a chapter to encourage the reader to continue on in the book. What are the cliffhangers at the ends of Chapters Fifteen and Sixteen?

_____

_____

_____

_____

III. *Building Suspense*—High interest in the outcome of a story is called suspense. The author builds suspense by placing the characters in danger, leaving the reader uncertain of the outcome. In what ways does the author build suspense?

_____

_____

_____

_____

Science Connection:

Do some research to learn about the life cycle of a moth or butterfly. Then write a letter to Doon explaining the change he noticed in his captive worm.

Music Connection:

What lullaby does Mrs. Murdo sing to Poppy? Do some research to find out more about lullabies. What were the first lullabies? What characteristics do all lullabies have in common?

Writing Activity:

Imagine you are a reporter covering the Singing for your newspaper. Write an article reporting on the days' events.

CHAPTERS 18 – 20

Vocabulary: Word analogies are equations in which the first pair of words has the same relationship as the second pair of words. For example, ATTRACTIVE is to UGLY as KIND is to CRUEL. Both pairs of words are opposites. Choose a word from the Word Box to complete each of the analogies below.

> *WORD BOX*
> catastrophes   fretful   refugees   unhurriedly
> expanse   infinitely   relentlessly

1. WISDOM is to KNOWLEDGE as AREA is to _____.

2. RUDELY is to POLITELY as _____ is to MERCIFULLY.

3. CONSIDERABLY is to _____ as JOYOUSLY is to HAPPILY.

4. _____ is to DISASTERS as EXAMINATIONS is to INSPECTIONS.

5. SELFISHLY is to GENEROUSLY as IMMEDIATELY is to _____.

6. DEFENDERS is to GUARD as _____ is to FLEE.

7. CALM is to _____ as CAUTIOUS is to RECKLESS.

> Read to learn what the children find at the end of their journey.

Questions:

1. Why is Lina terrified during the boat ride?

2. How do the children know when their boat journey ends?

3. How did Lina's lapse of memory create a problem for the citizens of Ember?

4. Why do the children think that their arrival has been expected?

5. What amazes the children most when they observe the landscape beyond the tunnel?

6. How do the children reveal that there were no birds in Ember?

7. Why did the builders tell the first residents of Ember to bring no books or photographs and say nothing ever again about their former world?

8. How do Lina and Doon reveal that there were no four-legged animals in Ember?

9. What do Lina and Doon conclude as they observe Ember from the cliff?

10. Why do Lina and Doon drop their message to Clary down to Ember?

Chapters 18 – 20 (cont.)

Questions for Discussion:

1. Why do you think the woman left her journal behind?
2. Why do you think that Stanley and the journal writer named their babies Star and Forest?
3. Describe the common animals and objects in the outside world with which Lina and Doon are unfamiliar. How do you think it would be to live in a world without these things?
4. What do you think Mrs. Murdo will do after reading the message?

Science Connection:

Doon and Lina see stalactites and stalagmites when the tunnel opens into a large room. Do some research to find out more about stalactites and stalagmites. What are they? How are they formed? Where are they found?

Literary Device: Figurative Language

Figurative language is writing not meant to be taken literally. This language is often used to create vivid impressions and help create a mood by setting up comparisons between dissimilar things. Similes, metaphors, and personifications are all forms of figurative language. Read the following excerpt:

> Lina felt as though a lid that had been on her all her life had
> been lifted off. Light and air rushed through her, making a
> song like the songs of Ember, only it was a song of joy.

How is figurative language used here to create vivid impressions? What mood does it help to set?

_____

_____

_____

Literary Element: Theme

A theme is a central idea or message that is carried throughout a book. Compile a list of important themes in the novel. Consider what the novel is saying about the following topics:

- personal strength and courage
- friendship
- the search for truth
- corruption
- responsibility
- inner demons

Writing Activity:

We know the thoughts and words of Lina and Doon after they leave Ember, but we have no idea what is happening back in the city. Imagine that Mrs. Murdo, concerned about Lina and Poppy, talks to Mr. Harrow. Write a dialogue between Mrs. Murdo and Mr. Harrow in which they discuss the missing children.

CLOZE ACTIVITY

The following passage has been taken from the Chapter Sixteen of the novel. Read it through completely. Then fill in each blank with a word that makes sense. Afterwards, you may compare your language with that of the author.

There was no flicker this time, just sudden, complete darkness. It was _____ [1] that Lina had already planned her move _____ [2] knew exactly which way to go. She _____ [3] up, knocking over her chair. With her _____, [4] she made a wide swipe and knocked _____ [5] the table next to the chair as _____. [6] The furniture thumping to the floor, the _____ [7] shattering, and the mayor's enraged shouts made _____ [8] clamor that covered the sound of her _____ [9] as she dashed to the stairway door. _____ [10] it unlocked? She reached for the knob. _____ [11] and squeaks told her that the mayor _____ [12] struggling to rise from his chair. She _____ [13] the knob and pulled, and the door _____ [14] open. She closed the door behind her _____ [15] leapt upward two steps at a time. _____ [16] in the pitch dark, she could climb _____. [17] In the room, the bell clanged and _____, [18] and the mayor bellowed.

When she got _____ [19] the first landing, she heard the guards _____. [20] There was a crash—someone must have _____ [21] over the toppled chair or table. "Where _____ [22] she?" someone yelled. "Must have run out _____ [23] door!" Did they know which door? She _____ [24] hear footsteps behind her.

If she could _____ [25] it to the roof—and if from _____ [26] roof she could jump to the roof _____ [27] the Prison Room and from there to the _____ [28]—then maybe she could escape. Her lungs were on fire now, her breath was burning her throat, but she climbed without stopping, and when she came to the top, she burst through the door to the roof and ran out.

POST-READING ACTIVITIES

1. Return to the Elements of Science Fiction chart that you began in the Pre-Reading Activities on page five of this study guide. Did you find an example of each of the elements? Compare your responses with those of your classmates.

2. Return to the character chart that you began on page twelve of this study guide. Complete the chart and compare your responses with those of your classmates.

3. Return to the conflict chart that you began on page seventeen of this study guide. Complete the chart and compare your responses with those of your classmates. Are there any conflicts left unresolved? If so, how do you think they will be resolved in subsequent books in the series?

4. What do you think will happen to Lina and Doon? Will Mrs. Murdo follow with the other citizens of Ember? Write a story line for a sequel to the book. Then read the chapter from *The People of Spark*, the actual sequel, at the end of the novel. Is it anything like your plot?

5. **Cooperative Learning Activity:** Imagine that you and a group of your classmates are going to make a film version of *The City of Ember*. In a cooperative learning group, do the following:
    *   List the scenes and events on which you want the film to focus. Indicate whether you will omit, add, or change any scenes.
    *   Make a list of the types of music that you think would be good background for the scenes you listed above.
    *   Cast the various roles and state the reasons for your choices.

6. Design a new cover for the novel. Make sure that the cover expresses an important aspect of the story.

7. Using a book of quotations such as *Bartlett's Familiar Quotations*, find a quotation that you think relates to *The City of Ember*. Copy the quotation and then write a paragraph explaining the connection.

8. People built the city of Ember because they feared the human race would not survive. In what ways did they miscalculate? Should Ember be abandoned, or can it be improved?

9. With your classmates, role-play any of the following hypothetical scenes:
    *   Doon's father defends his son against the mayor's accusations.
    *   Mrs. Murdo discusses the strange note she found with Clary.
    *   Lizzie tells Looper that Lina has found out their secret.
    *   Ten years after their escape, Lina attempts to describe the city of Ember to Poppy.

Post-Reading Activities (cont.)

10. Work with a classmate to create a letter that has whole words and parts of words missing. The letter should contain an important message or lead to a "treasure." Distribute copies of this letter to your classmates so that they can solve the mystery.

11. **Literature Circle:** Have a literature circle discussion in which you tell your personal reactions to *The City of Ember*. Here are some questions and sentence starters to help your literature circle begin a discussion.

    - How are you like Lina or Doon? How are you different?
    - Even though this book is science fiction, how are the characters realistic? How are they fantastic?
    - Which character did you like the most? The least?
    - Who else would you like to read this novel? Why?
    - What questions would you like to ask the author about this novel?
    - It was not fair when . . .
    - I would have liked to see . . .
    - I didn't understand . . .
    - I wonder . . .
    - Lina learned that . . .
    - Doon learned that . . .

12. Choose one of the questions that you wanted to ask the author above. Then go to her website at *http://www.jeanneduprau.com/index.shtml* and email the question to her.

SUGGESTIONS FOR FURTHER READING

Bawden, Nina. *Off the Road*. Penguin.

* Bradbury, Ray. *Fahrenheit 451*. Random House.

* Christopher, John. *The White Mountains*. Simon & Schuster.

Colfer, Eoin. *The Supernaturalist*. Hyperion.

Cooper, Susan. *Green Boy*. Simon & Schuster.

Farmer, Nancy. *The Ear, the Eye and the Arm*. Penguin.

Fox, Helen. *Eager*. Random House.

* Haddix, Margaret Peterson. *Among the Hidden*. Simon & Schuster.

_____. *Among the Imposters*. Simon & Schuster.

* L'Engle, Madeleine. *A Wrinkle in Time*. Random House.

* Lowry, Lois. *Gathering Blue*. Random House.

* _____. *The Giver*. Random House.

_____. *Messenger*. Random House.

Lyon, Steve. *The Gift Moves*. Houghton Mifflin.

McNaughton, Janet. *The Secret Under My Skin*. HarperCollins.

* O'Brien, O.T. *The Girl Who Owned a City*. Random House.

* O'Brien, Robert. *Z for Zachariah*. Simon & Schuster.

Paulsen, Gary. *The White Fox Chronicles*. Random House.

Philbrick, Rodman. *The Last Book in the Universe*. Scholastic.

* Sleator, William. *Interstellar Pig*. Simon & Schuster.

Some Other Books by Jeanne DuPrau

Car Trouble. Greenwillow.

Cells. Thompson Gale.

Earth House. Random House.

The People of Sparks. Yearling.

The Prophet of Yonwood (Book of Ember). Random House.

* NOVEL-TIES study guides are available for these titles.

ANSWER KEY

The Instructions, Chapters 1, 2
Vocabulary: 1. c 2. g 3. a 4. f 5. h 6. b 7. d 8. e; 1. frayed 2. disreputable 3. plummeting 4. successor 5. labyrinth 6. reverberating 7. endeavor 8. scavengers

Questions: 1. The builders put the instructions in a box with a timed lock set to open on the proper date. 2. The mayor of the city would keep the box without telling anyone about it. Then the first mayor would pass the box to the next mayor, and so on, all of them keeping it secret. 3. After taking ill, the seventh mayor took the box home and unsuccessfully tried to open it. After his death, the box ended up in the back of his closet, where it opened at the set time, with nobody aware of it. 4. Electricity is especially important because Ember is always dark except for the short times when electricity keeps the lights on. The problem is that the power lines and generator are so old that there are many blackouts. 5. The mayor comes to class because he would offer the oldest students, on the last day of their education, the opportunity to pick a career from the grab bag that he brought with him. Lina is disappointed with her grab bag choice because she has her heart set on being a messenger, and working in the Pipeworks is cold, dangerous work. 6. Doon changes jobs with Lina because he is sure that in the Pipeworks he can fix the generator and save the city. He also knows that Lina will want the job of messenger because she would not like working underground. 7. Lina is surprised by Doon's criticism because she had been taught that Ember was the only place of light in an otherwise dark universe. Having never been elsewhere, she thought the shabbiness and decrepit infrastructure of the city was normal. 8. No one in Ember can be absolutely certain of the day, week, or year because many of the time keepers throughout their history had been careless about keeping timepieces wound.

Chapters 3 – 5
Vocabulary: 1. raucous–loud and rowdy 2. turbulent–full of violent motion 3. chasm–deep opening or crack in the earth 4. attendance–state of being present 5. enmeshed–tangled up in 6. disagreeable–hard to get along with 7. incoherently–without making sense

Questions: 1. As a Pipeworks laborer, Doon discovers that not only are the lights about to fail and the supplies about to run out, but the water system is breaking down. 2. Doon's first look at the generator is disappointing because he cannot figure out how it works just by looking at it. 3. Doon wants to be the one to save the city in order to make his father proud of him. 4. Lina asks Mrs. Murdo to check up on her grandmother because she feared her growing forgetfulness: she had come home to find her grandmother tearing up the couch in search of an item she couldn't remember, and she had left the baby alone in the shop. 5. When Lina learns that there is a new job of trash sifter, she worries that the city of Ember may really be running out of everything. 6. Sadge is in a state of panic because he tried to venture into the Unknown Regions to find something that would help the people, but grew frightened of the complete darkness and returned. 7. Clary gives Lina a bean seed in order to help her appreciate the creation of life. 8. Lina has trouble finding Poppy because the lights go out and there is complete darkness. 9. Lina associates her desire for the colored pencils with her careless treatment of Poppy: if she had not selfishly desired the pencils, Poppy would not have wandered off and become lost in the darkened city.

Chapters 6 – 8
Vocabulary: 1. kiosks 2. incomprehensible 3. unintended 4. intact 5. disorderly 6. discontinued 7. illegible 8. ignited

Questions: 1. At the town meeting, the people react in anger and fear because they know the mayor is lying when he says that solutions are being found. 2. Lina thinks that the box contains something important because it is beautifully made and the writing on the paper is printed, just like the writing of the builders. She believes she will find instructions for a way to save the city. 3. Captain Fleery and the other Believers have faith in the builders who they know will return to save the city. 4. Most of the people of Ember cope with the shortages and blackouts by ignoring its seriousness and by putting the problems out of their minds. 5. Lina decides that Doon is the only person who might be interested in her document after she decodes the word *Pipeworks*. She then realizes that he is the perfect person to help her because he is curious, serious, and pays attention to things. 6. Certain that he will never understand electricity and be able to restore power to Ember by that means, Doon investigates the subject of fire: if he can harness the light from fire, he may be able to search the Unknown Regions.

Chapters 9 – 11

Vocabulary: 1. f 2. c 3. a 4. g 5. b 6. e 7. d; 1. unmistakable 2. delectable 3. sturdy 4. tainted 5. compartment 6. sauntering 7. methodically

Questions: 1. After studying Lina's document, Doon becomes excited, believing that it is indeed important. 2. Lina decides to go to the Pipeworks because Doon has found a door that she hopes will lead to something or someplace important. 3. Lina and Doon are disappointed at first when they cannot find the key to open the door, and then more disappointed when they see a man with a familiar gait let himself into the locked room and finally leave. 4. Granny calls Lina into her room in the middle of the night because she is dying and wants to be near her granddaughter. 5. Mrs. Murdo shows she is "somewhere between a friend and a relative" to Lina by inviting Lina and Poppy to live with her after Granny dies. 6. Since the seven-minute power outage, everyone in Ember seems worried: more and more people are sending messages expressing their concerns about the future. 7. Lizzie tries to avoid Lina because she is carrying bags full of canned goods that have been unavailable to others for a long time: she reluctantly reveals that Looper is her source for this bounty. 8. Lina refuses Lizzie's offer once she understands that it is Looper, the boy who sold her the pencils, who is supplying the food. Knowing that Looper resells scarce items at heavily marked-up prices, she believes it is an unfair practice and, although, tempted, will have nothing to do with this activity.

Chapters 12 – 14

Vocabulary: 1. S 2. A 3. S 4. A 5. A 6. S 7. S 8. A; 1. embedded 2. decipher 3. dim 4. slogans 5. egress 6. mottled 7. impatience 8. convoluted

Questions: 1. In the locked room, Doon discovers a room laden with supplies and the mayor asleep in the middle of everything. 2. It is getting harder for people in Ember to put the problem of failing electricity out of their minds because there are more and more blackouts, causing people to fear that the lights will go out for good. 3. As soon as Doon reveals to Lina that the locked room is full of supplies and that he saw the mayor there, Lina concludes that the man they saw coming out of the room was Looper: suddenly the message that Looper sent to the mayor through Lina— "Delivery at eight"—made sense. Looper is supplying the mayor with a treasure trove of supplies. 4. Lina realizes that Doon is her best friend when he shows sympathy and hugs her after hearing about Granny's death. 5. Lina goes to see Clary after she is disappointed that Doon has lost faith in the document. She wants to discuss the situation with someone who is sensible and trustworthy. 6. Clary gives Lina new hope when she tells her that *egress* means "the exit," indicating that the instructions indicate a way out of Ember. 7. Doon has trouble sleeping because he is excited by the information he and Lina deciphered in the fragments of paper found in the box. Knowing that the instructions might allow people to exit Ember, he is further excited by the possibility of announcing this to everyone during the Singing. 8. Doon and Lina discover boxes underground that contain objects that were at first alien to them, but later realized that objects labeled "matches" and "candles" would light their way down an otherwise dark tunnel. 9. Doon and Lina discover that the way out of Ember is on the river by boat.

Chapters 15 – 17

Vocabulary: Across–2. defying 4. rummaged 8. curtly 10. impudence 11. ponderously; Down–1. unfurled 3. accomplice 5. abundance 6. enraged 7. dispersing 9. tumult

Questions: 1. Doon decides to wait to tell his father about the way out of Ember because he wants the glory of having it announced at the Singing. 2. Suspecting that the guards are there to arrest Doon, Nammy Proggs purposely sends them in the wrong direction. 3. Doon and Lina, afraid that they will be caught by the guards and punished "for spreading vicious rumors," decide to go into hiding. They choose to hide in the school because it will be empty on the day of the Singing. 4. Lina cannot set her escape plan in motion immediately because the guards apprehend her as she leaves the school in order to bring a farewell message to Clary. 5. Lina manages to escape when the lights go out. She makes a dash for the stairway door and climbs to the roof. 6. Lina knows that Doon is on his way to the river because from a distance during the second blackout she sees a pinpoint of light moving at the edge of the crowd. She concludes that this is Doon carrying a candle. 7. With deep concern for his father, Doon leaves a farewell message for him and pins it to a kiosk where he hopes someone will deliver it. 8. Lina adds risk to her escape by bringing Poppy along.

Chapter 18 – 20

Vocabulary: 1. expanse   2. relentlessly   3. infinitely   4. catastrophes   5. unhurriedly   6. refugees   7. fretful

Questions: 1. Lina is terrified because the boat lurches and pitches wildly, she fears she may lose her grip on Poppy, and most of all, she fears the absolute darkness. 2. The children know when their boat journey ends because they reach a second pool with nowhere for the boat to go. After exploring, Lina finds a wide path. 3. Having forgotten to deliver her note to Clary, Lina realizes that no one in Ember would know what happened to Doon, Poppy, and herself, and that no one would know about the boats and the path they could take out of Ember. 4. The children realize that their arrival had been expected when they see a sign at the entrance to the path that began, "Welcome, Refugees from Ember!" 5. The children are amazed most by the moon and then the brightness of the rising sun. 6. When the children cannot identify the flying creatures with beautiful songs, it is clear that Ember must not have birds. 7. The builders wanted the babies to grow up with no knowledge of the world outside so that they would not feel sorrow for what they had lost. 8. Lina and Doon's encounter with the "creature" suggests that they have never seen common animals before. 9. As they see Ember below from the cliff in the cave, the children realize for the first time that Ember is underground. 10. Lina and Doon drop their message to Clary down the cliff in the hope that someone will appreciate its significance and use the instructions it contains to begin an exodus from Ember.